Shipwrecks

Written by
Cath Jones

When a boat or a ship sinks, it is called a shipwreck.

Most ships that sink at sea will stay on the sea bed for ever.

A ship might sink because something goes wrong on the ship. It might be something like a fire starting.

Sometimes, bad storms drive ships onto rocks. The rocks knock holes in the hull of the ship, which makes the ship sink.

Hundreds of years ago, a whole fleet of Spanish ships sailed into a storm. About twenty of the ships sank.

A long time ago, there were people known as **wreckers**. They wanted ships to hit the rocks and be wrecked.

They didn't think about the people on the ships. They just wanted to plunder the ships and take the things that were on them.

This is a painting of wreckers trying to grab loot from a wrecked ship. Can you see the wreckers standing on the rocky ledge?

Some ships are wrecked near the coast, where the sea is not deep. So we can still see those shipwrecks.

Some ships are wrecked in deep water, and some of these ships sink without trace. No one knows where they are.

Some people make it their job to hunt for shipwrecks. They know that if they can find the right shipwreck, they might get very rich!

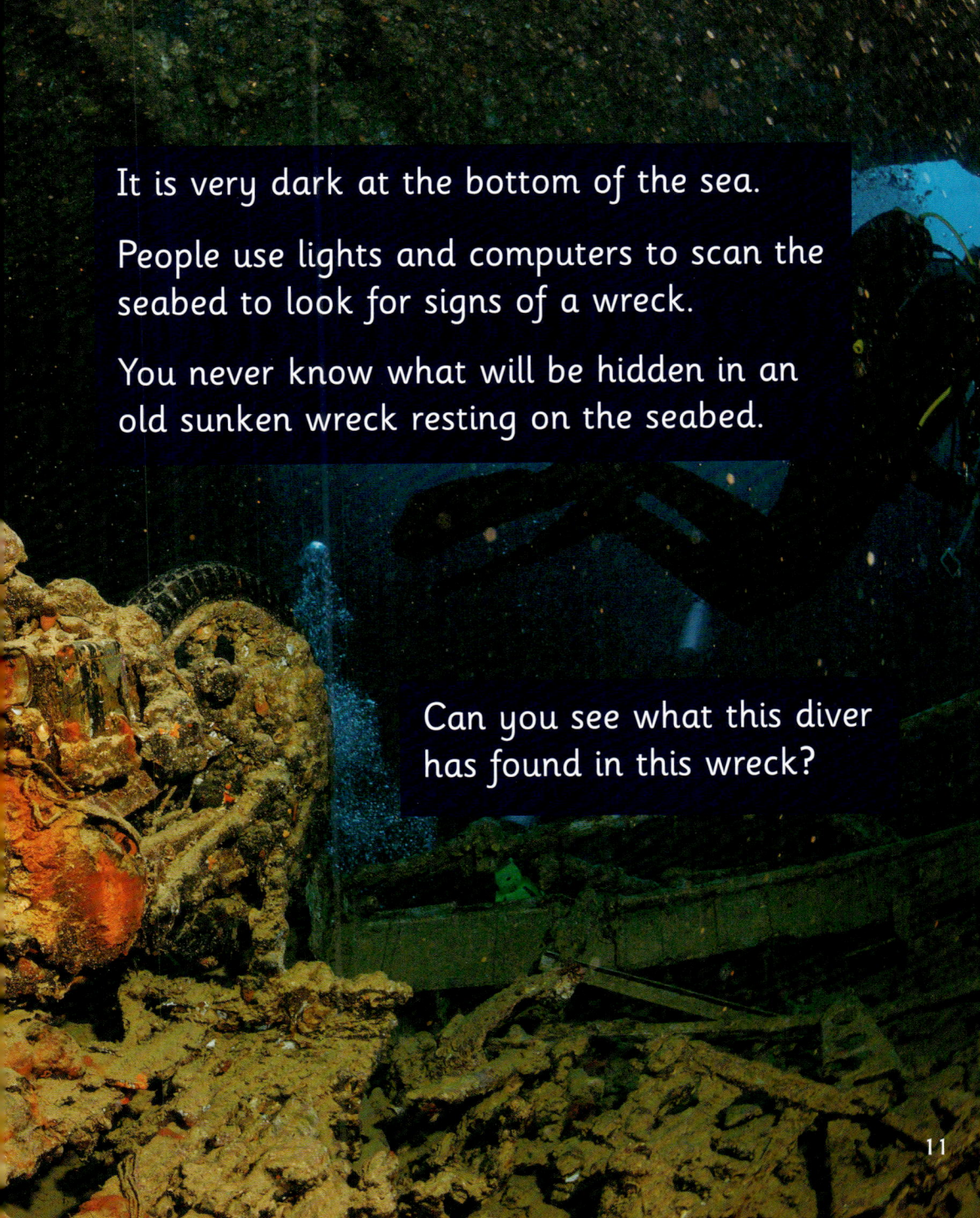

It is very dark at the bottom of the sea.

People use lights and computers to scan the seabed to look for signs of a wreck.

You never know what will be hidden in an old sunken wreck resting on the seabed.

Can you see what this diver has found in this wreck?

Many sea creatures make their homes on a shipwreck.

This ship sank over seventy years ago. Many different kinds of corals and fish have now made it their home. It looks as if the corals are climbing all over the wreck.

The wreck is glistening with so many bright reds, greens and blues!

Sometimes you can see wrecks without getting wet.

When there's a big storm, waves can sweep up a beach and shift the sand.

Long-lost wrecks can appear! Bits of wood poke out of the sand.

This is a wreck of an old wooden ship.

The things we find on a shipwreck can tell us how people lived in the past.

This case of glass is now a home for corals and fish. Visiting a shipwreck is like travelling back in time!